The Music of
JOHN DOWLAND
Made Easy for Solo Classical Guitar

Arranged and edited by Mark Phillips

ISBN: 978-0-9850501-8-4

A. J. Cornell Publicatio

CONTENTS

Come Again, Sweet Love

by John Dowland

3

Air

by John Dowland

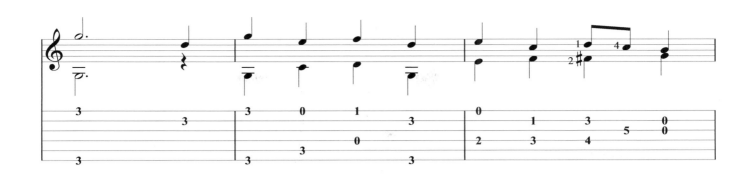

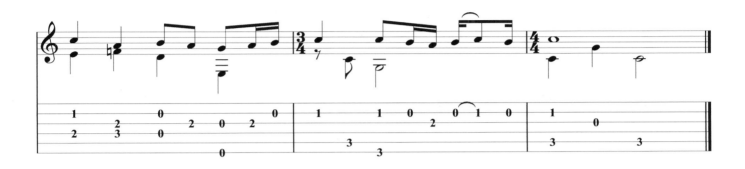

5

Clear or Cloudy

by John Dowland

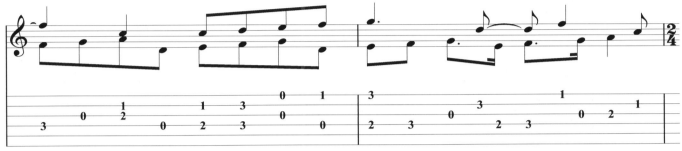

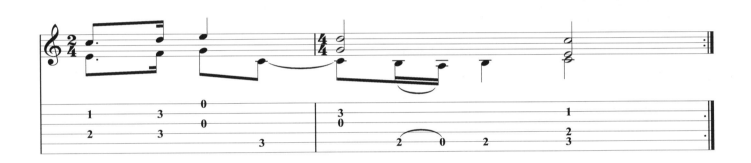

Flow, My Tears

by John Dowland

Moderately

Flow Not So Fast, Ye Fountains

by John Dowland

If My Complaints Could Passions Move

by John Dowland

Mrs. White's Nothing

by John Dowland

Brightly, in 2

White As Lilies Was Her Face

by John Dowland

Moderately fast

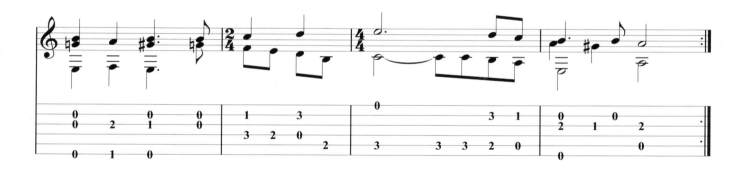

The Round Battle Galliard

by John Dowland

Tarleton's Resurrection

by John Dowland

Time's Eldest Son, Old Age

by John Dowland

Moderately

ABOUT THE COMPOSER

English lutenist and composer John Dowland was born in 1563. After studying for several years in France, Germany, and Italy, he earned the degree of Bachelor of Music from Oxford University in 1588; he afterwards received an honorary degree from Cambridge. Dowland was celebrated as the most accomplished lutenist of his age. He wrote much excellent music for his instrument, but is best known for his sets of lute songs, which are remarkable for their pathos. Of these, "Come Again, Sweet Love" and "Flow, My Tears" are among the best known. He also wrote instrumental music for solo lute, including galliards and pavanes. Dowland was appointed lutenist to King Christian IV of Denmark in 1597 and remained in His Majesty's service until 1609, after which he describes himself as "lutenist to the Lord Walden." In 1625 he was appointed one of the six lutenists to King Charles I. In 1609 he published an English translation of Andreas Ornithoparhcus's *Micrologus*, a work of great value to students of music theory. He died in 1626.

Made in the USA
Lexington, KY
21 December 2016